One Simple Thing That Changes Everything in Your Business

ACTION GUIDE & WORKBOOK

Learn the Must-Haves to Kick Start Real Change in Your Business (and Life!) and Have Everything That Matters

Beverly Boston

North America's #1 Real Estate, Sales Coach and Mentor

"I had no idea that being your authentic self could make me as rich as I've become. If I had, I'd have done it a lot earlier."

~ Oprah Winfrey

DEDICATION

This actionable workbook is dedicated to small thinking.
May it rest in peace!

DREAMS & VISIONS FROM THE PAST

My three biggest dreams and goals to grow my business are:

1. _____

2. _____

3. _____

I am most proud of these three things while fulfilling my dreams and goals to grow my business:

1. _____

2. _____

3. _____

The three most noteworthy ways I am better fulfilling my dreams and goals to grow my business:

1. _____

2. _____

3. _____

If I could start and do it again, I would do these three things to fulfill my dreams and goals in a different way to grow my business:

1. _____

2. _____

3. _____

The three greatest lessons I've learned about fulfilling my dreams and goals around growing my business, so far are:

1. _____

2. _____

3. _____

The three greatest influences that have impact on my while fulfilling my dreams and goals around growing my business:

1. _____

2. _____

3. _____

The three greatest successes of the past year in fulfilling my dreams and goals around growing my business:

1. _____

2. _____

3. _____

The three greatest setbacks in fulfilling my dreams and goals of the past year around growing my business:

1. _____

2. _____

3. _____

Three personal improvements I've made towards fulfilling my dreams and goals around growing my business in the past year are:

1. _____

2. _____

3. _____

If I could go back and do it again, I would do these three things differently to fulfill my dreams and goals around growing my business from the last year:

1. _____

2. _____

3. _____

The three greatest lessons I've learned in the last year are to fulfill my dreams and goals around growing my business:

1. _____

2. _____

3. _____

The three greatest influences that had the biggest impact on my in my business growth over the last year were:

1. _____

2. _____

3. _____

The three best decisions I made last year around my business growth were:

1. _____

2. _____

3. _____

The three risks I took last year to fulfill my dreams and goals were:

1. _____

2. _____

3. _____

The three greatest contributions I made to others in my business to fulfill my dreams and goals over the last year were:

1. _____

2. _____

3. _____

The three most important business relationships to me over the last year were:

1. _____

2. _____

3. _____

The three habits that have worked well for me over the last year to fulfill my dreams and goals were:

1. _____

2. _____

3. _____

The three habits that have not worked well for me over the last year to fulfill my dreams and goals were:

1. _____

2. _____

3. _____

CURRENT DREAMS AND VISIONS

The three things I need to do less of in the next year to fulfill my dreams and goals are:

1. _____

2. _____

3. _____

The three things I need to do more of in the next year to fulfill my dreams and goals are:

1. _____

2. _____

3. _____

The three things I need to stop doing altogether in the next year to fulfill all of my dreams and goals are:

1. _____

2. _____

3. _____

The three reasons that I believe I can succeed in fulfilling bigger dreams and goals are:

1. _____

2. _____

3. _____

Three of my main assets (skills, attitude, and personality) that will help me achieve bigger dreams and goals are:

1. _____

2. _____

3. _____

The three things I need to do to build my confidence and overcome my fears to dream bigger are:

1. _____

2. _____

3. _____

Three business owners or sales professionals who have succeeded but do not have the same assets you do, or to the degree that you do:

1. _____

2. _____

3. _____

Three great gifts of unique talents and skills I have been given are:

1. _____

2. _____

3. _____

Three ways I can use these great gifts of knowledge and experience to fulfill my daring big dreams and goals are:

1. _____

2. _____

3. _____

If I doubled or tripled those goals and dreams they would now be:

1. _____

2. _____

3. _____

Three ways in which I will find support fulfilling my big dreams and goals are:

1. _____

2. _____

3. _____

Three ways in which I will take action now to start fulfilling my dreams and goals:

1. _____

2. _____

3. _____

Three ways in which I will overcome any obstacles that get in my way:

1. _____

2. _____

3. _____

Where do I want to be in one year from now?

_____

_____

_____

_____

_____

_____

Three ways I will know I have succeeded and fulfilled my dreams and goals:

1. _____

2. _____

3. _____

29 Things to Stop Hiding and Playing Small that Business School Did Not Teach You

Before you can begin this process of transformation you have to stop doing the things that have been holding you back, and stop playing small and hiding out. Come out and shine!

These are tips that you won't get in business school! Here's a checklist of things to STOP before you get STARTED:

1. ## Stop spending time with the wrong people in your business.

   A business life is too short to spend time with people who suck the joy out of you. If someone wants to be a part of your business growth, they'll make room for you. You shouldn't have to fight for a spot. Never, ever spend time with someone who continuously overlooks your worth. And keep in mind: it's not the people who stand by your side when you're at your best, but the ones who stand beside you when you're at your worst that are your true supporters in growing your business.

2. ## Stop running from your business problems.

   Face up to them. No, it won't be easy. There is no realtor or agent in the world capable of flawlessly handling every blow thrown at them. We aren't supposed to be able to instantly solve problems. That's not how we're made. In fact, we're made to get upset, sad, hurt, stumble and have a few bumps in the road. That's the whole purpose of being alive – to face problems, learn, adapt, and solve them over the course of time. This is what ultimately creates us into the successful sales professionals we become.

3. **Stop "BS-ing" yourself.**

You can lie to anyone else in the world, but you can't lie to yourself. Our sales improve only when we take chances, and the first and most difficult chance we can take is to be honest with ourselves.

4. **Stop putting your own needs last.**

The most painful thing is losing yourself in the process of giving too much, and forgetting that you are extraordinary too. Yes, help others; but help yourself too. If there was ever a moment to follow your passion and do something that matters to you, that moment is now.

5. **Stop trying to be someone you're not.**

One of the greatest challenges in business is being yourself in a world that's trying to make you like everyone else. Avoid becoming the "mini-me" of someone else. Someone will always be prettier, someone will always be smarter, someone will always be younger, someone will always be more successful but they will never be you. Don't change so people will like you. Be yourself and the right buyers, colleagues and others will love the real you.

6. **Stop trying to hold onto the past.**

You can't start the next chapter of your business or dare to dream big dreams if you keep re-reading your last one.

7. **Stop being scared to make a mistake.**

Doing something and getting it wrong is at least ten times more productive than doing nothing in business. Triple your mistakes and double your success. Every successful business has a trail of failures behind it, and every failure is leading towards success. You end up regretting the things you did NOT do far more than the things you did.

8. Stop beating yourself up for old mistakes.

We may choose the wrong business partner and complain about how so many things went wrong, but no matter how things go wrong, one thing is for sure, mistakes help us find the right business partner and things that are right for us. We all make mistakes, have struggles, and even regret things in our past. But you are not your mistakes, you are not your struggles, and you are here NOW with the power to shape your day and your future. Every single thing that has ever happened in your business is preparing you for a moment that is yet to come.

9. Stop trying to buy happiness.

Many of the things we desire are expensive. But the truth is, the things that really satisfy us are totally free – love, laughter, and working on our passions as we fulfill our daring big dreams and goals.

10. Stop exclusively looking to others for happiness.

If you're not happy with who you are on the inside, you won't be happy in business with clients, colleagues or others either. You have to create stability in your own mind and business first before you can share it with someone else.

11. Stop being inactive.

Don't think too much or you'll create a problem that wasn't even there in the first place. Evaluate situations and take decisive action. You cannot change what you refuse to confront. Making progress involves risk, period! You can't make it to second base in your business with your foot on first.

12. **Stop thinking you're not ready.**

   Nobody ever feels 100% ready when an opportunity arises to grow their business. Most great opportunities in business force us to grow beyond our comfort zones, which means we won't feel totally comfortable at first.

13. **Stop getting involved in business relationships for the wrong reasons.**

   Business relationships must be chosen wisely. It's better to be alone than to be in bad company. There's no need to rush. If something is meant to be in your business, it will happen – in the right time, with the right person, and for the best reason. Grow your business when you're ready, not when you're desperate.

14. **Stop rejecting new business relationships just because old ones didn't work.**

   In business you'll realize that there is a purpose for everyone you meet. Some will test you, some will use you and some will teach you. But most importantly, some will bring out the best in you.

15. **Stop trying to compete against everyone else.**

   Don't worry about what others are doing better than you. Concentrate on beating your own records every day. Success is a challenge between you and yourself only.

16. **Stop being jealous of others.**

   Jealousy is the art of counting someone else's blessings in their business instead of your own.

17. Stop complaining and feeling sorry for yourself.

Business curveballs are thrown for a reason – to shift your path in a direction that is meant for you. You may not see or understand everything the moment it happens, and it may be tough. But reflect back on those negative curveballs thrown at you in the past. You'll often see that eventually they led you to a better place, person, state of mind, or situation. So smile! Let everyone know that today you are a lot stronger than you were yesterday, and you will be.

18. Stop holding grudges.

Don't run your business with hate in your heart. You will end up hurting yourself more than the people you hate. Forgiveness is not saying, "What you did to me is okay." It is saying, "I'm not going to let what you did to me ruin my happiness forever." Forgiveness is the answer… let go, find peace, liberate yourself! And remember, forgiveness is not just for other people, it's for you too. If you must, forgive yourself, move on and try to do better next time.

19. Stop letting others bring you down to their level.

Refuse to lower your standards to accommodate those who refuse to raise theirs in business.

20. Stop wasting time explaining yourself to others.

Your colleagues, clients and others don't need it and your enemies won't believe it anyway. Just do what you know in your heart is right for you and your business.

21. **Stop doing the same things over and over without taking a break.**

The time to take a deep breath is when you don't have time for it. If you keep doing what you're doing, you'll keep getting what you're getting. Sometimes you need to distance yourself to see things clearly.

22. **Stop overlooking the beauty of small moments.**

Enjoy the little things, because one day you may look back and discover they were the big things. The best portion of your business will be the small, nameless moments you spend smiling with someone who matters to you.

23. **Stop trying to make things perfect.**

The real business world doesn't reward perfectionists; it rewards people who get things done.

24. **Stop following the path of least resistance.**

Business is not easy, especially when you plan on achieving something worthwhile. Don't take the easy way out. Do something extraordinary.

25. **Stop acting like everything is fine if it isn't.**

It's okay to fall apart for a little while. You don't always have to pretend to be strong, and there is no need to constantly prove that everything is going well. You shouldn't be concerned with what other people are thinking either – cry or smack some pillows if you need to – it's healthy. The sooner you do, the sooner you will be able to smile again.

26. Stop blaming others for your troubles.

The extent to which you can achieve your daring big dreams and goals depends on the extent to which you take responsibility for your business success. When you blame others for what you're going through, you deny responsibility – you give others power over that part of your business.

27. Stop trying to be everything to everyone.

Doing so is impossible, and trying will only burn you out. But making one person smile can change the world. Maybe not the whole world, but their world. So narrow your focus.

28. Stop worrying so much.

Worry will not strip tomorrow of its burdens, it will strip today of its joy. One way to check if something is worth mulling over is to ask you this question: "Will this matter in one year's time? Three years? " If not, then it's not worth worrying about.

29. Stop focusing on what you don't want to happen.

Focus on what you do want to happen. Positive thinking is at the forefront of every great success story in business. If you awake every morning with the thought that something wonderful will happen in your business today, and you pay close attention, you'll often find that you're right.

Business Growth UPGRADE Checklist for the New Successful Woman

Are you ready to grow your business, increase your sales, and become The New Successful Woman? Is everything in place for you to attract and help more buyers than you can handle (a great problem to have)? Do you have a systematic approach for marketing and sales that will attract ideal potential buyers? The following 10 questions provide a checklist to see if you're ready:

1. Do you have a clearly defined destination?

It's not much fun to do a lot of work growing your business only to realize that you're not happy where you've ended up. Develop a crystal clear vision and purpose for your business. For example, how many ideal potential buyers do you want? How much revenue do you want or need this year? What types of buyers are ideal for your agency? Your goals and strategies will flow much easier from a place of clarity.

2. Do you know who your ideal buyer is and what specific benefits and solutions you're offering?

What is the profile of your ideal potential buyer? What problems do they have that would make them want to hire you? What are the specific benefits and solutions you can give them that exactly meets their needs? What types of ideal potential buyers would you really enjoy working with? Getting clear on what you're selling and who you're selling to will make it easier for you to focus on qualified ideal leads and make it easier for ideal potential leads to find you!

3. Can you clearly establish and communicate what sets you apart?

Get clear on what makes you different from others who do what you do. Do you have a unique approach, process or model that you utilize? Maybe you're a specialist or an expert in a particular niche. Your track record or customer list may be what sets you apart. You must answer the question "Why should I specifically hire you versus someone else?" even if your ideal potential client doesn't openly ask it.

4. Do you have a marketing message that gets attention and interest, and keeps it?

When someone asks you "What do you do?" do you answer in a way that identifies the problems you solve or the benefits and solutions you provide? Do you engage the listener in an interactive dialogue where they want to know more rather than uttering a rehearsed commercial?

5. Do you have a way to keep in touch and further qualify ideal potential buyers?

Do you have a way to keep in front of your ideal potential buyers on a regular basis? So much of success in sales depends on timing. Treat client attraction marketing as a process rather than an event. Stay visible to the ideal potential buyers and continue giving them information to help them get comfortable and excited with the idea of working with you. Then when they have a need, you'll be top of mind.

A great tool is a newsletter or e-zine, or a blog where you can provide valuable information. Further qualify your ideal potential clients by offering a free report and excellent content. Those who request it are most likely worth following up with first.

6. Do you have a follow-up strategy that invites buyers or sellers to set up an appointment or presentation?

It's been said "the gold is in the follow up." If you're not systematically following up with ideal potential buyers or sellers, you're missing out on massive business growth. You can invite the ideal lead to explore working with you by phone, mail, e-mail, e-zine, any social media sites, etc.

7. Do you have a method of structuring a conversation that simultaneously builds rapport and enables you to thoroughly understand the needs of your market?

Once the ideal potential buyer or seller is in front of you, do you have an approach to understand their needs BEFORE you present your solution? An ideal lead won't hire you unless they know, like and trust you. How can they trust you if you haven't taken the time to fully understand their challenges and explored with them a desired result?

8. Does your approach include giving leads an offer they can't refuse?

Do you give the ideal potential buyer or seller a compelling offer that motivates them to take action? I've seen countless brochures, blogs, sales pages, blogs and websites that leave this part out. Along with the promise of great results, do you offer a free appointment or presentation, or a guarantee to reverse the risk? Think about how you can make your invitation completely irresistible!

9. Are you providing such great service that referrals naturally flow your way?

Are you providing extraordinary value to your current clients so that they want to refer you and you are actually earning and deserving of those referrals? Do you consistently deliver great results?

10. Do you have a winning mindset, leaving success no place to hide?

Do you have the tenacity, persistence and wherewithal to execute your business development and growth plan? If you do, you realize that business development and growth takes an investment of time, energy and money. You're willing to make that investment and stay the course in the good times and the bad.

So how did you do? Are there items on the checklist that are missing from your client attraction marketing and ability to become The New Successful Woman? Are there other items that need to be upgraded? A little improvement in each of these areas will significantly enhance your business development and growth results.

Checklist for Busy Saleswomen
10 Tips for Better Time Management, Efficiency and Organization

1. "Bookend" your day with growth planning and organization.

When you start your day with a plan and an organized office, you are able to hit the ground running and accomplish so much more. Each morning, review and revise your "to do" list. At the end of the day straighten up your workspace and create your schedule for the following day.

2. Focus on the most important task at hand.

Women are natural multi-taskers, but its hard to do more than one task well at a time. Put your energy into doing one thing right and move on to the next thing when you are done. If necessary, keep a running list of what needs to be done as new tasks show up.

3. Set aside a block of uninterrupted time during the day.

Let everyone in your office or virtual team know that you are unavailable for phone calls, appointments or questions during this time. Use your undisturbed time to reorganize or for catching up on tasks you usually don't have time for.

4. Take control of your email.

Delete emails on a regular basis, check email only at designated intervals, and keep as little in your in-box as possible.

5. Develop a "short call" mindset.

Politeness is expected in business conversation, but you can still make briefness your intention without being inconsiderate. Replace, "How are you?" with "How may I help you?" Open-ended questions like, "How are you?" invite lengthier responses.

6. Establish clear boundaries for how long you will allow meetings to last.

The key to an effective (and brief) meeting is preparation. Let everyone know ahead of time how long the meeting will last, the topics that will be addressed, and the information you expect each person to contribute.

Stick to the plan and discourage sidetracking.

7. Make a single page list of frequently called phone numbers and post it near your phone.

It takes more time than you realize to look up a number on your computer or rolodex. Have the numbers you need most often at the tip of your dialing finger.

8. Group similar tasks for maximum efficiency.

Returning phone calls, answering emails, writing personal notes, and running errands are all categories of tasks that are done more easily if grouped together. When you make one phone call it is easier to just keep moving down the list.

9. Keep separate in-boxes for different categories of papers.

Try separating your papers into these categories: items that are immediate and important; items that are "on hold" or pending; and items that are ready to be filed, passed on to someone else or reviewed at a later time. Keep the in-boxes on a surface near your desk.

10. Keep your desk clutter-free.

Keep your stapler, tape dispenser, extra pens and other supplies in a drawer rather than on top of your desk. Display photos, awards and knickknacks on walls or shelves, and reserve the top of your desk for the essentials - your telephone, computer, and today's work.

Wealth & Prosperity Mindset Checklist

In order to build a wealth and prosperity mindset to dare to dream bigger, you need to equip yourself with the physical, emotional, and spiritual tools necessary to stay the course. Reflect on the statements below each day to maintain a healthy mind, body, and spirit.

- ▶ I focus on positive pursuits.

- ▶ I am grateful for all that I have.

- ▶ I focus on the belief of an overflowing of abundance.

- ▶ I choose to have a positive opinion of myself.

- ▶ I refuse to wallow in setbacks – I rise to the challenge.

- ▶ I expand my comfort zone through daily challenges.

- ▶ I am focused on where I am and want to go.

- ▶ I challenge the false perceptions that limit my success.

- ▶ I believe that I am worthy of success, wealth and prosperity.

- ▶ I am open to new opportunities, even if it appears overwhelming.

- ▶ I take bold, consistent actions every day.

- ▶ I am confident about my abilities and talents.

- ▶ I focus my attention on enjoying each moment of my life journey.

A Business Mindset Reality Check

Principle #1: Face up to what you need to in your business to create change and transformation

Strategy: Become a sales professional who is transparent with you. Find out what makes you tick, keep what you like, and change the rest. Learn why you do what you do, and don't do what you don't. This principle is so fundamental in its truth that you should treat it as a personal challenge in developing your business growth.

Principle #2: You Generate Your Own Experiences

Strategy: Come clean and accept accountability for your current business results. Understand your role in creating the results in your business. Learn how to choose better so you have better. The principle is simple: you are accountable for your current business results. Good, bad or ugly, successful or unsuccessful, happy or sad, prosperous or broke, fair or unfair, you own your business results.

Principle #3: Successful Sales Professionals Do What Works

Strategy: Discover the payoffs that drive your behaviours. Control the payoffs to control those behaviours. Sadly, some behaviours, often the ones which we most hate and want to eliminate, are the very ones that tenaciously continue to occur in your business again and again.

Principle #4: You Cannot Change What You Do Not Come Clean About

Strategy: Get transparent with yourself about your current business situation and everybody in it and around you. Be brutally honest about what isn't working in your business. Stop making excuses, hiding out and playing small. Start making changes and transformations that create improved results and allow you to thrive.

Principle #5: Business Growth Rewards Fast Action

Strategy: Make careful decisions and then take fast action. Dreams become a reality not only with words, but also with fast actions. The reply, reactions and results that you get from others, in any situation, are triggered by the incentive you provide. The incentives are your behaviours. Improve those and your sales improve too.

Principle #6: Your Reality is Only Your Perception

Strategy: Distinguish the lens through which you view the world around you. Is it positive or negative? Big thinking or small thinking? Come clean about your past mistakes, poor choices and fears in business without being inhibited by them. This principle is so profound that it determines whether or not you are joyful, satisfied, and at peace in your business.

Principle #7: Business Is Meant to Thrive; It's a Process

Strategy: Learn to take charge of your business results, and own them. This is a long ride, and you are behind the wheel every day. Simply put, never in the life of your business are you without problems, fears, difficulties and challenges. Learn to work through them.

Principle #8: You Teach Customers and Others How Act Towards You

Strategy: Own, rather than grumble and criticize about, how customers, colleagues and others act towards you. Learn to renegotiate your business relationships to have what you want and deserve in your business.

Principle #9: Get Clear, and then Name Your Daring Big Dreams and Goals

Strategy: Get crystal clear about what you want, dare to dream big, and then go for it. This principle means what it says in the most basic sense. If you cannot name what you want, and name it with clarity and specifically, then you will never be able to step up and have it all.

Big Business Growth Readiness Checklist

Use this checklist to determine if your business is ready for BIG change and the growth you desire. Rate each consideration on a scale of 1-5, 5 being the most favourable or positive. If you do not meet the 5 standard, write the necessary steps to ensure this consideration is dealt with.

1. Is there a clear statement of required change?

2. Are positive consequences for change (and negative consequences for the absence of change) well described?

3. Have similar changes been successful in the past?

4. Are both informal and formal team members prepared to carry the message?

5. Does your team display your agility and readiness for change (lead by example)?

6. Is the business focused on specific elements of change (to avoid too much going on at the same time)?

7. Has the business shown a "constancy of purpose" to counter the element of resistance that says, "We'll just wait this out and it will pass"?

8. Are key people and sub-groups supportive of the change?

9. Are team members taken care of when change disrupts the business and employment opportunities?

10. Are people properly trained for new work requirements?

11. Do appropriate avenues for communication exist?

12. Do team members see a need for change?

13. Do team members feel they have a stake in the outcome?

14. Is technology (or other required infrastructure) in place to accommodate the change?

15. Are potential risks well defined?

16. Are strategies in place to minimize any adverse impact of known risks or unintended consequences?

17. Have team members shown their innovative and creative ability in the past?

18. Do leaders understand how team members and other stakeholders gauge success?

19. Do team members trust the media and other known forms of getting information?

20. Do team members generally trust each other?

21. Is the team's outlook for the future aligned with the business' goals and objectives?

22. Do team members share information in a timely and accurate way?

23. Do incentives and rewards exist that will recognize those who lead and support change?

24. Can the business admit mistakes?

25. Are team members empowered to become part of positive business change?

26. Can creativity and the potential for future progress co-exist with pride in the past and present (not seen as criticism and condemnation)?

27. Is change a common element of success and ingredient for advancement in the business?

Readiness for Big Business
Growth Checklist

Are you really ready for big business growth? This is a critical determination to make. Below are several questions to guide you now. Next to each question, indicate whether you believe your business is really ready. The final determination is up to you. If you're not ready yet, use the considerations in the right-hand column to determine how you might get ready and when you might be able to begin your project. This checklist will be useful to you whether you are a one-woman show or a team.

Answer each readiness question with a "yes, I'm ready" or "no, I'm not ready." In each instance you feel not ready, determine what needs to be done to be ready.

1. Do you have sufficient funds budgeted for the project? How can you get funds in time to start a project soon?

2. Do you have the time to participate in a major project for big business growth? How can you find the time to participate in a project like this?

3. Are you open to perspectives other than your own about the project? How can you become more open to other perspectives?

4. Are you open to hearing specifically about what might be your own role in any issues found in the business? How can you become more open to hearing about your own role?

5. Have you gone for outside help such as from mentors or coaches and had success before? If difficulties were experienced, what were they? How can your project avoid those experiences?

6. Are all-important people invested in creating big business growth? If there are important people not invested, who are they? How will they get involved in the project?

7. Can you, the leader, be assured of access to necessary people and business growth activities for the project? If not, how will you get access to those people?

8. Are all-important people comfortable with the project? If there are people who would be uncomfortable, what should be done?

9. Do you, knowing what you know now, feel that you are really ready for a project to create big business growth? Are there any "red flags," or feelings of concern on your part? If there are, what are they? How can they be addressed?

10. Do you feel that your business mindset is really ready for major change and business growth? Are there any "red flags" or feelings of concern on your part? If there are, what are they? How can they be addressed?

Thriving or Surviving Checklist

Are you barely making it? Having a tough time? While fulfilling your daring big dreams, thriving is a goal. But what does thriving look like?

Virtually all of the practices listed on this checklist are proven practices that facilitate mental and physical well-being.

DAILY PRACTICES

Laughing in delight

Being playful with others

Getting good sleep

Being physically active

Mindfulness

Attending to the beauty of the natural world

Eating well and enjoying healthy food

Expressing creativity (such as: cooking, writing, playing music, singing, writing poems)

Caring for others and being cared for when you need it

Practicing gratitude

GENERAL PRACTICES

Confiding in at least one close friend (most days)

Not succumbing to temptations too frequently (like dessert!) and learning not to feel tempted

Maintaining practices that foster positive self-development-learning to prefer what is good and healthy

Finding a mentor or coach for areas where you want to improve

Knowing how to let go and put annoying things in perspective

Find ways to gradually increase in effectiveness and competence for the things you want to accomplish (take small steps; chip away)

SOCIAL LIFE

Having at least one close loving relationship (after learning to appreciate closeness)

Having a group of people on whom you could rely if needed

Having at least one confidant who can help you over rough patches

Taking risks to connect to and help others

Mentoring others with whatever knowledge, skills and wisdom you have

Doing kind things for others whenever you can

Making amends with those you have wronged or who have wronged you

FEELINGS

Feeling like you are making a valuable contribution to the community

Feeling like others care for you (practice compassionate meditation that starts with compassion towards yourself)

Being in touch with your heart feelings

Using healthful ways to calm yourself down from anxieties, fears, and angers

Forgiving yourself and others

Doing things that create good feelings in yourself instead of angry or contemptuous feelings

GOALS AND MOTIVATION

Waking with a positive purpose that reaches beyond yourself

Meaningful work or activity outside your business

Feeling connected to your community

Feeling in relationship to other lives in the natural world

These activities and strivings help you along the path to fulfilling your big daring dreams and goals.

You might have additions based on what helps you thrive. Or perhaps you thrive on some days and not on others. What is the difference?

On the days I don't thrive, sometimes it is because I am taking in too much the sad state of the world. In that case, I need to get back to focusing on what I can do to make things better, one moment at a time. But usually when I have a non-thriving day it is because I am beating myself up for not achieving some goal I thought I should have achieved or worrying about an outcome I can't control. These obsessive downers bring to mind the serenity prayer, which is also about learning to thrive:

God/Universe/Spirit grant me the serenity to accept the things I cannot change, the courage to change the things I can, and the wisdom to know the difference.

We can all change ourselves by choosing to increase our thriving.

That may be the first step to changing the world.

Give Voice to Your Values Checklist

This exercise is designed to help you give voice to your values and clarify your vision for success.

Step 1: What I Value Most...

From this list of values (both work and personal), select the ten that are most important to you-as guides for how to behave, or as components of a valued way of life and fulfilling your daring big dreams and goals while growing your business. Feel free to add any values of your own to this list.

Achievement | Advancement and promotion | Adventure
Affection (love and caring) | Arts

Challenging problems | Change and variety | Close relationships | Community
Competence | Competition | Cooperation | Country | Creativity

Decisiveness | Democracy

Ecological awareness | Economic security | Effectiveness | Efficiency
Ethical practice | Excellence

Fame | Fast living | Financial gain | Freedom | Friendships

Growth

Having a family | Helping other people | Helping society | Honesty

Independence | Influencing others | Inner harmony | Integrity
Intellectual status | Involvement

Job tranquility

Knowledge

Leadership | Loyalty

Market | Meaningful work | Merit | Money

Nature

Order (tranquility, stability, conformity)

Personal development | Physical challenge | Pleasure | Power and authority
Privacy | Public service | Purity

Quality of what I take part in | Quality relationships

Recognition (respect from others, status) | Religion | Reputation
Responsibility and accountability

Security | Self-respect | Serenity | Sophistication | Stability
Status | Supervising others

Time | Truth

Wealth | Wisdom | Working under pressure | Working with others
Working alone

Step 2: List Your Ten Values Here:

1. _____

2. _____

3. _____

4. _____

5. _____

6. _____

7. _____

8. _____

9. _____

10. _____

Step 3: Elimination

Now that you have identified ten, imagine that you are only permitted to have five values. Which five would you give up? List the ones that you would keep here:

1. _____

2. _____

3. _____

4. _____

5. _____

Now imagine that you are only permitted four. Which would you give up? Cross it off. List the four you would keep here:

1. _____

2. _____

3. _____

4. _____

Now cross off another, to bring your list down to three. Then cross off another, to bring your list down to two. List the two you would keep here:

1. _____

2. _____

Finally cross off one of your two values. Which is the one item on the list that you care most about? List it here:

1. _____

Use this guidepost, a beacon for when you feel lost or unsure about the direction you are going in while fulfilling your dreams and goals.

Fixed vs. Growth Mindset

Which Way Do You Lean?

Throughout the book I referred to fixed mindset vs. growth mindset. It is such an important topic and critical piece to whether or not you will succeed that I am focusing a bit more on it here.

Here is a piece from an article about Carol Dweck, a professor of psychology at Stanford University:

Through more than 3 decades of systematic research, [Carol Dweck] has been figuring out answers to why some people achieve their potential while equally talented others don't—why some become Muhammad Ali and others Mike Tyson. The key, she found, isn't ability; it's whether you look at ability as something inherent that needs to be demonstrated or as something that can be developed.

To anyone who is into growth and self-improvement, this seems evident. But clearly, it is not clear to everybody. Take a look at this diagram by Nigel Holmes indicating the two types of mindsets and I'll sure you'll be familiar with the attitudes of many business owners, colleagues, and others you know, including yourself.

Fixed Mindset

Let's start with the Fixed Mindset:

People who hold these beliefs think that "they are the way they are", but that doesn't imply that they have less of a desire for a positive self-image than anyone else. So of course they want to do well and look smart. But to achieve these goals…

By definition, a challenge is hard and success is not guaranteed, so rather than risk failing and negatively impacting their self-image, they will frequently steer clear of challenges and keep with what they know they can do capably.

This is same with obstacles. The difference here is that challenges are things that you can choose to do while obstacles are outside forces that get in your way.

What's the point of working hard and making efforts if afterward you are still at the same place that you started or even stuck? If your view of the world tells you that effort is a distasteful thing that doesn't really pay off, then the smart thing to do is to stay away from it as much as possible.

Constructive negative feedback is often ignored, and taken as an insult in some cases. Having the Fixed Mindset logically leads you to believe that any criticism of your abilities is direct criticism of you. This typically discourages the people around you and after a while they give up handing you any negative feedback, further isolating you from outside influences that could create some change and even transformation.

The success of others is seen as a standard against which the person looks bad or inferior. Typically when others succeed, people with a Fixed Mindset will try to convince themselves and the people around them that the success was due to either being lucky (after all, almost everything is due to luck in the Fixed Mindset) or objectionable actions. In some cases, they will even try to taint the success of others by bringing up things that are completely unrelated that detracts from that success.

As a result, they don't reach their full potential and their beliefs feed on themselves and can grow out of control. They don't change or improve much with time, if at all, and so to them this confirms that "they are as they are" and they were right all along.

Growth Mindset

Let's now look at the Growth Mindset:

People who hold the Growth Mindset believe that intelligence can be developed, and that the brain is like a muscle that can be trained over time. This leads to the desire to advance and improve.

And how do you improve and advance? First, you embrace and even welcome challenges, because you know that you'll come out stronger on the other side of that growth.

Likewise, obstacles – outside setbacks – do not discourage you. Your self-image is not tied to your success and how you will look to others; failure is an opportunity to learn, and so whatever happens you win and the upside is that you move closer to your dreams and goals.

Effort is seen not as something useless to be avoiding but as necessary to grow and master useful skills.

Criticism and negative feedback are sources of information and something to learn from. That doesn't mean that all criticism is worth incorporating or that nothing is never taken personally, but at least the Growth Mindset individual knows that he or she can change and improve, so the negative feedback does not seem as being directly about them as a person, but rather about their current abilities.

The success of others is seen as a source of inspiration and information to learn from. To Growth Mindset individuals, success is not seen as a zero-sum game.

And so, Growth Mindset individuals will improve and this will create a positive feedback loop that encourages them to keep learning and improving and of course fulfilling any big dreams and goals.

What's Next?

The good news – in particular if you just recognized yourself as being someone who holds the Fixed Mindset view, is that it is possible to change from one to the other.

What's more, Carol Dweck has shown that people can learn to adopt the latter belief and make dramatic strides in performance.

Does the Fixed vs. Growth Mindset theory fit with your personal experience? Does it describe the people around you? Which one do you lean towards?

Change from Fixed to Growth Mindset

Step 1. Learn to hear your fixed mindset "voice."

As you approach a challenge, that voice might say to you "Are you sure you can do it? Maybe you don't have the gift or genius," "What if you fail?—you'll be a failure," "Colleagues will laugh at you for thinking you had gifted or genius," "If you don't try, you can protect yourself and keep your pride."

As you hit a setback, the voice might say, "This would have been easy if you really had gift or genius," "You see, I told you it was a risk. Now you've gone and shown the whole planet how limited you are," "It's not too late to back out, make excuses, and try to regain your pride."

As you face criticism, you might hear yourself say, "It's not my fault. It was something or someone else's fault." You might feel yourself getting angry at the person who is giving you feedback. "Who do they think they are? I'll show them." The other person might be giving you specific, constructive feedback, but you might be hearing them say "I'm really disappointed in you. I thought you were competent but now I see you're not."

Step 2. Recognize that you have a choice.

How you interpret challenges, setbacks, and criticism is your choice. You can interpret them in a fixed mindset as signs that your fixed gifts or genius or abilities are lacking. Or you can interpret them in a growth mindset as signs that you need to ramp up your strategies and effort, stretch yourself, and expand your abilities. It's up to you.

So as you face challenges, setbacks, and criticism, listen to the fixed mindset voice and...

Step 3. Talk back to it with a growth mindset voice.

As you approach a challenge:

THE FIXED-MINDSET says
"Are you sure you can do it? Maybe you don't have the genius or gift."

THE GROWTH-MINDSET answers,
"I'm not sure I can do it now, but I think I can learn to with time and effort."
FIXED MINDSET: "What if you fail—you'll be a failure"

GROWTH MINDSET
"Most successful professionals had failures along the way."

FIXED MINDSET
"If you don't try, you can protect yourself and keep your pride."

GROWTH MINDSET
"If I don't try, I automatically fail. Where's the pride in that?"

As you hit a setback:

FIXED MINDSET
"This would have been an easy if you really had genius or gift."

GROWTH MINDSET
"That is so wrong. Basketball wasn't easy for Michael Jordan and science wasn't easy for Thomas Edison. They had a passion and put in tons of effort."

As you face criticism:

FIXED MINDSET
"It's not my fault. It was something or someone else's fault."

GROWTH MINDSET
"If I don't take responsibility, I can't fix it. Let me listen—however painful it is– and learn whatever I can."

Then...

Step 4. Take the growth mindset action.

Over time, which voice you heed becomes pretty much your choice. Whether you

- take on the challenge wholeheartedly,

- learn from your setbacks and try again, or

- hear the criticism and act on it is now in your hands.

Practice hearing both voices and practice acting on the Growth Mindset. See how you can make it work for you.

Grow Your Business:
Action Habit Checklist

Sales professionals that dare to dream big dreams share one quality — they get things done. This ability supersedes intelligence, talent, and connections in determining the size of your salary and the speed of fulfilling your dreams and goals.

Despite the simplicity of this concept there is a perpetual shortage of real estate and sales professionals who excel at getting the kinds of results I have been speaking about throughout this book. The action habit — the habit of putting ideas into action now — is essential to getting things done and accomplishing what we have been talking about. Here are 7 ways you can grow the action habit:

1. Don't wait until conditions are perfect

If you're waiting to start until conditions are perfect, you probably never will. There will always be something that isn't quite right. The timing is off, the market is down, or there's too much competition. In the real world there is no perfect time to start. You have to take action and deal with problems as they arise.

List what you need to start now:

2.   Be a doer

Practice doing things rather than thinking about them. Do you want to start using social media as a client attraction tool? Do you have a great idea to develop a product? Do it today. The longer an idea sits in your head without being acted on, the weaker it becomes. After a few days the details get hazy. After a week it's forgotten completely. By becoming a doer you'll get more done and stimulate new ideas in the process.

List what you need to do now:

3.   Remember that ideas alone don't bring success

Ideas are important, but they're only valuable after they've been implemented. One average idea that's been put into action is more valuable than a dozen brilliant ideas that you're saving for "some other day" or the "right opportunity". If you have an idea that you really believe in, do something about it. Unless you take action it will never go anywhere.

List what new ideas you can implement now:

4.   Use action to cure fear

Have you ever noticed that the most difficult part of public speaking is waiting for your turn to speak? Even professional speakers and actors experience pre-performance anxiety. Once they get started the fear disappears. Action is the best cure for fear. The most difficult time to take action is the very first time. After the ball is rolling, you'll build confidence and things will keep getting easier. Work through your fear by taking action and build on that confidence.

List what fears you need to overcome now:

5.   Start your creative engine mechanically

One of the biggest misconceptions about creative work is that it can only be done when inspiration strikes. If you wait for inspiration to slap you in the face, your work sessions will be few and far between. Instead of waiting, start your creative motor mechanically. If you need to write something, force yourself to sit down and write. Put pen to paper. Brainstorm. Doodle. By moving your hands you'll stimulate the flow of ideas and inspire yourself.

List where your business creativity needs to happen now:

6. Live in the present

Focus on what you can do in the present moment. Don't worry about what you should have done last week or what you might be able to do tomorrow. The only time you can affect is the present. If you speculate too much about the past or the future you won't get anything done. Tomorrow or next week frequently turns into never.

List where you're still focusing on the past in your business:

7.   Get down to business immediately

It's common practice for sales professionals to socialize and make small talk at the beginning of meetings. How often do you check email or blogs before doing any real work? These distractions will cost you serious time if you don't bypass them and get down to business immediately. By becoming someone who gets to the point you'll be more productive and people will look to you as a leader.

List where you need to get down to business now:

It takes courage to take action without instructions from anyone else. Perhaps that's why initiative is a rare quality that's coveted by business owners and executives everywhere. Seize the initiative. When you have a good idea, start implementing it without being told. Once others see you're serious about getting things done they'll want to join in. The people at the top don't have anyone telling them what to do. If you want to join them, you should get used to acting independently, until you decide to get a mentor or coach to catch your blind spots. We all have them, and doing so will save you time, money and energy to fulfill your daring big dreams.

Your Values, Vision & Growth Checklist

The turning point in my business came when I discovered and learned that everything happens for a reason. I discovered while mentoring and coaching thousands of business owners that daring to dream big dreams and having consistent success is not an accident. A lack of success is not an accident either. I also discovered that business owners who are highly successful in any area of their business more often than not are those who have learned the cause-and-effect relationship between what they want and how to really get it.

1. Have You Established Your Business Growth and Development Values?

To realize your full potential for personal and professional growth and development, begin with your values as they apply to your own gifts, talents and abilities. As you know, your values are expressed in your words and actions. You can tell what your values are by looking at what you do and how you respond to the world around you. Your values are the root causes of your motivations and your behaviours.

List them here:

2. Have You Refined Your Business Growth and Development Vision?

Create a long-term vision for yourself in the area of business growth. Plan ahead for the next five or ten years and imagine that you are developed fully in every important part of your business. Idealize and see yourself as outstanding in every area you deem important. Simply refuse to compromise on fulfilling your daring big dreams.

List them here:

3. Have You Created Specific Goals for Your Business Growth and Expansion?

Now take your vision and develop it into specific goals. Here is a great way to get started now: in the space below write down 10 goals that you would like to achieve in the area of personal and professional development in the months and years to come. Write in the present tense, just as if you were already the sales professional you intend to be.

Decide exactly what you want to be able to do. Decide who you want to become. Describe exactly what you will look like when you become truly outstanding in your business and in your personal life.

4. Have You Upgraded Your Knowledge and Skills?

Establish specific methods for each of your goals. If your goal is to be outstanding in your business, decide how you will know when you have achieved it or arrived at your chosen destination. Decide how you can gauge your growth and assess your success.

Perhaps you can use as a gauge the number of hours you are mentored in a week. Perhaps you can gauge the number of books you read or the programs you dive into and complete. Perhaps you could gauge your growth by the number of new clients you get, as result of creating a new strategic client attraction plan.

List how you will gauge your success here:

5. Have You Developed Winning Business Growth Habits?

Choose the specific habits, action and behaviours you will need to rehearse and prepare daily to become the realtor or agent you want to be. These could be the habits of clearness, being focused, preparation, and attention to detail, solid work ethic, resolve, and persistence.

List these habits here:

Luminary Legacy Checklist

Writing a luminary legacy statement goes much further than describing the actions or symbols you are most proud of. That is the stuff left for obituaries and such. Luminary legacy statements focus more on the characteristics and values for which you would most like to be remembered, and that you will live, breathe and model.

Creating a luminary legacy statement entails a number of steps

1. Reflect and ponder

2. Find the consistent themes in your reflections and pondering

3. Write the statement

4. Elicit reaction

5. Revise, amend and rework the statement

6. Frequently review, reflect and update

Soul Searching Questions

1. How do you wish to be remembered by those in and around your business, both in your current role and in your profession as a whole? For which two or three personal characteristics (or skills, behaviours, or values—choose the word that feels right or makes the most sense for you) would you most like to be remembered? How would you like to have these characteristics manifest themselves? How will they show up? You might want to briefly describe a situation or even a recollection of you that someone might have in the future. Remember, what we write down is more likely to become our reality than if we did not.

2. What have you learned in this position, your business, and your life thus far that you would most like to pass on? Be specific

3. How will you express or pass on that learning?

4. What remains to be accomplished? Why is that important in building, growing or completing your luminary legacy?

5. Apart from more time, what will help, block or get in the way of you in completing what remains to be accomplished?

FREE BONUSES

KICK-START REAL CHANGE AND GROWTH TODAY!

How do smart real estate and sales professionals think and grow rich while making a difference?

Smart people take action.

Get started today, by downloading Beverly's popular *Business Breakthroughs Kit*. This popular kit includes FREE access to her award-winning Breakthroughs Assessment, Breakthroughs Dynamic ebook and the Smart People's Achievement Formula.

http://beverlyboston.com/actnow

About the Author

Beverly Boston will guide and train you to help more people, market better, get more clients, and have more sales–with less time, less effort and less energy.

Four Seasons Hotels, UBC, Labinal, Masco, Bank of America, Royal Bank, Dominion Lending, REMAX, Coldwell Banker, Prudential, Century 21 Weichert, MacDonald, Sutton, Sotheby's, Keller Williams, Long & Foster, Royal LePage, Dexter, and many more think of me as an expert in the big arena for smart real estate and sales professionals-the real business world.

With over 17,000 hours (and counting) of coaching, training, and mentoring as well as 3 decades of study and research into what makes real estate and sales professionals successful–I keep it real and relevant.

I help sales professionals, realtors, and mortgage brokers obtain freedom from being stuck & broke in a self-employed mindset, to an executive mindset by delegating, automating and replicating systems to building an empire with a visionary and luminary outlook and make meaningful change in the world. One of my clients increased her income by 10.6 times over in just a few months.

If you want to turn potential leads into clients and sales, or still struggling to get any business–you're in the right place.

Learn more about Beverly

http://beverlyboston.com/